MW00564582

FLY TYER'S GUIDE TO
TYING ESSENTIAL
BASS AND PANFISH FLIES

FLY TYER SERIES

FLY TYER'S GUIDE TO
TYING ESSENTIAL
BASS AND PANFISH FLIES

Jerry Darkes

LYONS PRESS
An imprint of Globe Pequot Press
Guilford, Connecticut

To buy books in quantity for corporate use
or incentives, call **(800) 962-0973**
or e-mail **premiums@GlobePequot.com.**

Copyright © 2014 Jerry Darkes

ALL RIGHTS RESERVED. No part of this book may be reproduced or transmitted in any form by any means, electronic or mechanical, including photocopying and recording, or by any information storage and retrieval system, except as may be expressly permitted in writing from the publisher. Requests for permission should be addressed to Globe Pequot Press, Attn: Rights and Permissions Department, PO Box 480, Guilford, CT 06437.

Lyons Press is an imprint of Globe Pequot Press.

All interior photos by Jerry Darkes

Project editor: Staci Zacharski
Text design and layout: Sue Murray

Library of Congress Cataloging-in-Publication data is available on file.

ISBN 978-0-7627-9183-5

Printed in the United States of America

10 9 8 7 6 5 4 3 2 1

CONTENTS

Introduction viii

Chapter 1: The Big Picture 1
The Fish 1
The Waters and the Equipment Used 9
Flies 12

Chapter 2: Getting Started 15
Necessary Tools 15
    Vise 15
    Scissors 18
    Bobbin 19
    Hackle Pliers 20
    Bodkin/Half-Hitch Tool 21
Other Useful Tools 22
    Bobbin Threader 22
    Whip Finisher 22
    Hair Stacker 23
    Hair Packer 23
    Tweezers 23
The Tying Area 24
Materials 25
    Hooks 26
    Thread 27

Body Materials 28

Feathers 30

Tails, Hairs, and Furs 31

Synthetic Hair and Flash 34

Eyes, Heads, Weight, and Legs 35

Foam 38

Chapter 3: Basic Techniques 41

Starting the Thread 41

Wrapping the Thread 43

Finishing Off the Thread 44

Weighting a Body 46

Tying in Barbell Eyes 48

Making a Hook Weedless 50

Making the Whip Finish 52

Chapter 4: Below the Surface 55

The Sinking Spider 56

The Woolly Bugger Family 58

The Sinking Spider Variation 59

The Basic Woolly Bugger 59

The Better Bugger Variation 62

The Damsel/Dragon Variation 65

The Baitfish Bugger Variation 67

Bead-Head or Cone-Head Variation 68

The Hellgrammite Variation 70

Simple Crayfish 70

Sculpin Bugger 72

The Deep Minnow Family 74

The Basic Deep Minnow 74

Spottail Shiner Variation 77

Perch Minnow Variation 78

Jig Deep Minnow 78

Simple Minnow 79

Crafty Minnow 79

Fish Head Minnow 80

Chapter 5: On the Surface 81

Floating Spider/Ant 83

Poppers 85

Simple Popper 85

Instant Popper 87

Blockhead Popper 89

Simple Slider 91

Divers 92

Rabbit Strip Diver 92

Hairy Diver 94

A Dynamic Duo 95

Froggy Diver 95

Froggy Popper 98

Index 102

About the Author 104

INTRODUCTION

In this age of the Internet, with all of the world's knowledge at our fingertips, it may seem that a beginner's fly-tying guide is unnecessary. In fact, the opposite is more likely true. There is so much information available to us that it often overwhelms the beginner. The purpose of this guide is to give a novice tyer the basic information needed to tie productive patterns for our most widely distributed sport fish—bass and panfish.

In this guide I will review the primary fish species that fall under the "bass and panfish" umbrella, take a look at the various types of waters where these fish are found, and discuss the equipment and flies used for these fish. The major portion of this book will then review the tools, materials, and techniques needed to tie flies that will catch these fish.

I will introduce the concept of "fly templates." These are basic, proven, fish-catching designs. Once a design template is mastered, we can then make adjustments or changes within the template to create a new pattern or adapt a pattern to a new set of conditions or circumstances. By following this format, flies can be tied for bass and panfish (and nearly all species) that will be productive under a complete range of angling situations. I will present several established templates for both surface and subsurface patterns along with variations of them.

In addition, recent advances in materials, tools, and techniques of use to the beginning tyer will be presented. I have worked to meld the old with the new—that is, to include a series of proven, fish-catching pattern templates with both new materials and ideas, giving the flies a fresh look.

Fly tying to me is a journey of creativity and learning. The best part of this activity is that the creativity and the learning never ends. My goals are to give the beginning tyer the information to tie essential flies for bass and panfish and also expose the experienced tyer to new ideas and materials.

Chapter 1

The Big Picture

The Fish

A general discussion of bass and panfish needs to include an assortment of species. The best-known species are largemouth and smallmouth bass, along with bluegill and sunfish. These are all popular targets for fly anglers. Interestingly, both the largemouth and smallmouth bass are actually members of the sunfish family, along with crappie and rock bass. The true bass are relatives of the saltwater striped bass. The best known of these in freshwater is the white bass, also called the silver bass.

One final addition to the panfish category would be the yellow perch. Though not always targeted on flies, they are often caught while fishing for other species, and make an interesting addition to the panfish category.

All of these fish are referred to as warm-water species. By this definition, we mean that they prefer water temperatures over 60 degrees Fahrenheit. This can be a bit misleading as we find that some of them, such as smallmouth bass and yellow perch, can tolerate a wide range of temperature extremes. However, most will make seasonal movements to stay in their preferred comfort range.

The largemouth bass (*Micropterus salmoides*) is one of the most widely distributed freshwater sport fish and the runaway favorite of American anglers. It is found in forty-nine of the fifty states (not Alaska), across parts of southern Canada, parts of northern and central Mexico, and into Cuba and Puerto Rico. It has also been transported to Europe, Japan, Australia, and South Africa. There are two subspecies of largemouth bass—the northern strain and the Florida strain. The

Largemouth bass are well distributed across North America and beyond. They are a great target for fly anglers and eagerly strike surface patterns.

average largemouth will weigh 1 to 3 pounds across most of their range, but the Florida strain can grow in excess of 20 pounds.

Largemouth are generally found in ponds and lakes, but may also inhabit slower moving areas of rivers. They prefer soft-bottom areas with aquatic vegetation and a variety of structure, including trees and logs. They are opportunistic feeders and are willing to consume a wide variety of prey, including baitfish such as shiners and shad, panfish, frogs, and other aquatic organisms. If it will fit in its mouth, a largemouth may try to eat it. Largemouth can also be selective feeders at times if there is an abundance of a particular organism, such as damselflies or just-hatched fry, available.

Largemouth bass are greenish in color with darker blotches that form a horizontal line across their body. The upper jaw, when closed, extends back beyond their eye. Their sensory system allows largemouth to feed effectively in a wide variety of water conditions, including at night. Largemouth are best known to fly anglers for their explosive strikes on the surface, but, as we shall see, they also respond very well to subsurface fly patterns.

The smallmouth bass (*Micropterus dolomieu*) continues to gain popularity as a top fly-rod target. They are native to the eastern United States, Canada, and the Great Lakes region. Stocking programs have distributed them to all states except Alaska. They tend to be smaller in size than largemouth bass but make up for it in fighting ability. Many anglers consider smallmouth, pound-for-pound, the toughest of all freshwater fish.

Smallmouth bass can inhabit a wide range of waters, including lakes, reservoirs, rivers, and creeks. They will tolerate a much wider range of water temperatures than largemouth and prefer a bottom with a harder substrate such as sand, gravel, and broken-up rock. They feed

Smallmouth bass hit flies readily and are great sport on a fly rod. They can be caught in creeks, rivers, and lakes across much of the United States and Canada.

primarily on baitfish and crayfish but will also target various insects. This is especially true in moving water situations where hellgrammites (dobsonfly larvae), dragonflies, and damselflies are found. Smallmouth may become very selective feeders at times, requiring a fly that closely resembles the available forage. This is especially true in clear-water situations.

Smallmouth range in color from greenish bronze to almost black, depending on their environment. Fish from the tannic rivers of the upper Midwest and southern Canada are often very dark, while those from clearer waters are much lighter colored. Smallmouth have broken vertical color bars across their side, which often "light up" when they get excited. The upper jaw, when closed, extends to, but not past, the eye. Across much of their range, smallmouth bass are also called "smallies" or "bronzebacks."

Several other bass species may also be encountered by fly anglers. The spotted bass (*Micropterus punctulatus*) is found across the central and lower Mississippi drainage. Also called the Kentucky bass or just "spot," it exhibits coloration similar to a largemouth, but the lower jaw does not extend past the eye. Spotted bass also have a patch of teeth on their tongue, while the tongue of a largemouth is smooth. Spots prefer habitat more similar to that of smallmouth bass.

The Coosa bass, shoal bass, and Guadalupe bass are also members of the sunfish family. They are smallmouth-like in coloration and characteristics, but inhabit small ranges in the southern United States.

The true sunfish include common species such as the bluegill (*Lepomis macrochirus*); redear sunfish (*Lepomis microlophus*), also called shellcracker; warmouth (*Lepomis gulosus*); and rock bass (*Ambloplites rupestris*). Additional fish within the family include the colorful longear sunfish (*Lepomis megolotis*) and green sunfish (*Lepomis cyanellus*). Of these, the bluegill and possibly the rock bass present the best opportunities for fly anglers.

Bluegills are found across much of North America and have been transplanted to various locales around the world. They are the panfish most commonly targeted by fly anglers. In the southern United States,

Bluegill, a fly rod, and a Floating Spider make for an ideal fly-fishing combination.

bluegills are often called bream or "brim." Bluegills thrive in both lakes and ponds as well as slow-moving river systems. They are normally found close to underwater vegetation and cover.

Bluegills feed on a variety of organisms, including aquatic insects, crustaceans, and even small fish. This makes them receptive to a wide range of fly patterns. Bluegills are most often targeted in the late spring and early summer when they are concentrated in large groups, spawning. After spawning, larger specimens often suspend over deeper water, making them difficult to locate, but they will still move into shallower areas to feed early in the morning and late in the day. Bluegills have a small mouth, so flies for them need to be downsized to consistently hook them.

Most bluegills will weigh 6 to 10 ounces, but specimens over a pound are frequently caught, especially in the southern parts of their

Bluegills on spawning beds present a perfect fly-fishing opportunity.

range. During spawning they are voracious, and will attack nearly anything that comes close to them. At other times they can be very selective feeders, often targeting specific aquatic larva.

Rock bass are found in faster-moving rivers and streams, as well as lakes with a hard or rocky bottom. They are often caught by anglers targeting smallmouth bass, as both species frequent similar areas. Also called goggle-eye or "redeye," rock bass are well distributed across the Great Lakes and Saint Lawrence systems and south to the mid–Mississippi River basin.

Rock bass feed on smaller fish, insects, and crustaceans. Their mouths are quite large relative to the size of their body, allowing them to attack fairly large flies. As their name implies, rock bass prefer areas with rock-strewn structure. They nest and spawn in shallow areas.

Crappie are a popular target of anglers in many areas across North America, but not a regular catch for most fly fishers as they tend to stay

A common panfish species, rock bass love to hit flies that resemble their favorite food—crayfish.

in water over 10 feet deep except when spawning. There are two species, the white crappie (*Pomoxis anularis*) and black crappie (*Pomoxis nigromaculatus*). Both species are often referred to as speckled perch or just "specks." They are most often encountered while spawning in shallow areas adjacent to flooded brush and timber. However, their nesting areas tend to be deeper than other panfish. Crappies favor small baitfish but will also feed on aquatic insects and crustaceans.

Yellow perch (*Perca flavescens*) are another very popular panfish, but not generally targeted by fly fishers. They tend to be bottom feeders, although larger specimens may be encountered while working subsurface patterns for smallmouth bass. Most yellow perch are found in larger lakes and reservoirs. They are considered the finest eating of the panfish and support a substantial commercial fishery in parts of the Great Lakes.

White bass (*Morone chrysops*) are a native freshwater species of the true bass family—Moronidae. They are found across much of the

A hybrid between a white bass and a striped bass, wipers reach large size and are excellent fighters. They will hit flies in many situations.

Midwest from southern Ontario to Oklahoma, being especially abundant in Lake Erie and down through much of the Mississippi River basin. They are generally open-water residents but become targets of fly anglers when they ascend tributaries and shallow reef areas to spawn. Huge schools of white bass will feed on emerald shiners and other baitfish, and will readily hit flies that imitate this forage, becoming great sport for fly anglers.

White bass are also called silver bass and sand bass. They average around 12 inches in length and a pound in weight. They have been crossbred with striped bass by fish managers in hatcheries, resulting in hybrids that are known as "wipers" or sunshine bass. These hybrids can reach sizes in excess of 20 pounds and are a popular sport fish where they are stocked.

White perch (*Morone americana*) are not a true perch but rather a member of the temperate bass family, Moronidae. They are native to eastern North America, from Nova Scotia south into the Carolinas, often being found in brackish areas. They are an invasive species in the Great Lakes and have been found to compete with both yellow perch and white bass. They will also hybridize with white bass where their ranges overlap.

THE WATERS AND THE EQUIPMENT USED

The classic image of fly fishing for bass and panfish has the angler at a farm pond on a warm evening in early summer. In this scenario, surface patterns are cast on a floating line to fish cruising the shallows or spawning. This is certainly an enjoyable situation, and it's the way many of us, myself included, were introduced to fly fishing. However, it is far from the only opportunity we have to tangle with these fish on fly-fishing equipment.

The various fish species described earlier inhabit a wide range of waters, from tiny ponds and small streams to big rivers, large lakes and reservoirs, and even the waters of the Great Lakes. As our equipment has advanced, so has our ability to target fish with flies in a wide range of situations. In many cases, we now have the ability to mimic many of the presentations that conventional anglers make.

On most waters, smaller panfish will be easily handled on a 5-weight outfit. The rod can range anywhere from 8 to 9 feet in length. A longer rod is often preferable for higher backcasts when walking shorelines with high grass. A shorter rod may be better suited for small stream work when casting in tight quarters or from a canoe or kayak where the shorter length makes landing fish easier.

The most common line will be a weight-forward floater. In temperate areas, a standard trout line will suffice. If fishing in hot weather, look for a line that is tailored toward warmer temperatures. This line will maintain its firmness and cast better than a cold-water line that may get too soft and become difficult to cast.

A standard trout leader of 7½ to 9 feet tapered to 3X or 4X will suffice. This will give a breaking strength at the tippet of 6 to 8 pounds. Keep this as strong as possible, as a sizable largemouth will invariably grab a fly intended for a smaller target. There are times, though, when a lighter tippet may be needed, such as when fishing clear, calm water in bright sunshine.

The reel can be a simple, single-action design. In most cases, it simply serves as a line-holding device. Panfish can usually be stripped in without the need to put the line on the reel. Add backing as needed to fill the line spool. This helps minimize coiling when the line is on the reel for a period of time.

If planning to work a range of depths, a sinking-tip or even full-sinking line may be needed. Although a long leader and weighted fly can be allowed to sink, the fly will creep toward the surface on the retrieve. When a portion of the line also sinks, the fly will be held at depth for a much longer period of time. Modern sinking lines are precision tools, with both the length of the sinking section and the sink rate well defined. With a bit of use, the angler knows where the fly is at all times.

Anglers can use outfits as light as 3-weights for smaller panfish but need to be aware of the limitations. Flies will need to be kept small—#10 and smaller—to cast effectively. Also, any amount of wind will make casting extremely difficult. Finally, the light rod makes it very difficult to keep any sizable fish away from cover.

Smallmouth bass are found in a wide range of environments, from small streams to larger rivers, from man-made reservoirs to the Great Lakes. In small stream situations, where the average fish is 8 to 10 inches long and the flies are fairly small, a 5-weight outfit may be fine. Flies may have a bit of weight or air resistance to them, but a 5-weight line can usually carry them. The size of the fish often increases with the size of the water fished, however, and fly size and line weight should also increase accordingly. In medium-size and larger rivers, a 6-weight outfit would be the minimum, though a 7-weight setup would be better. The 7-weight line will handle a much wider range of fly sizes without being too powerful for smaller fish. It is my favorite line for most river smallmouth fishing.

When moving to open-water situations such as the largest rivers, reservoirs, or lakes, I like an 8-weight outfit. This 8-weight line allows anglers to throw a wide range of fly sizes and push a line into the wind. This line is easier to cast for distance and allows one to cover more water. In addition, the heavier rod allows larger fish to be landed easier, reducing their stress.

In rivers, one can expect a good amount of surface and near-surface activity, so a floating line is used much of the time. Taper designs specific to bass fishing allow heavier and more air-resistant flies to be cast easier. All manufacturers make lines of this style. The most recent designs to aid anglers are integrated shooting-head lines such as Scientific Anglers' Titan Taper or the Rio Outbound. The Titan Taper also has a dimpled finish on it that reduces line friction in the guides and makes picking the line up off the water easier.

On larger water, sink-tip and sinking-head lines will significantly increase the fly angler's success. The ability to hold a fly at certain depth for an extended period is crucial. Scientific Anglers' Wet Tip Express and Steamer Express lines along with the Rio Outbound can help maximize fish-catching opportunities on bigger water. These lines provide the ability to effectively fish flies to depths of around 20 feet. Again, all manufacturers make similar-style lines. I've had experience with the ones listed.

When using a floating line for smallmouth, a bass taper leader with a breaking strength of 10 pounds is a good starting point. Smallmouth are rarely leader shy, and this type of leader has a heavier butt section, allowing flies to be turned over more efficiently. With sink-tip and sinking-head lines, I usually attach a 1-foot butt section of 20-pound-test monofilament to the line and then loop tippet onto it. The tippet section is usually 3 to 5 feet long and normally 12-pound test.

When specifically targeting largemouth bass, the 8-weight outfit is a starting point. Again, this allows a very wide range of fly sizes and weight to be cast efficiently. In addition, it provides power to keep fish from diving into the nearest cover. As largemouth are normally caught in, or close to, aquatic vegetation or sunken timber, leaders need to be strong and the rod needs to have lifting power to move fish.

The standard rig for largemouth would be a floating bass taper line and leader tapered to 12-pound at the tippet. This will suffice for most pond and small lake situations. On larger lakes and reservoirs, the sinking-head line also comes into play. It is most enjoyable to experience the explosive strike of a largemouth on the surface, but these opportunities often have a limited time frame. Fishing below the surface opens up a whole new dimension for catching bass on a fly.

For both smallmouth and largemouth, rods should again be 8 to 9 feet. The wading or walking angler will likely choose the longer rod, while the shorter rod is often easier to use from a watercraft, especially when trying to control and land an active fish. There are also rods available just under 8 feet in length to be legal for tournament use. Echo, Redington, and Sage all market rods of this style.

For both smallmouth and largemouth bass, the reel can again be a simple single-action. On larger water, having a functional drag on the reel becomes important, as other species may be incidentally encountered. Carp, channel catfish, and freshwater drum will all take flies intended for bass. The big difference is that these fish often take off on a powerful run as soon as they are hooked. A working reel drag can keep the reel from overrunning and minimize skinned knuckles.

In extreme situations, such as targeting southern largemouth in heavy cover and casting large flies, one might need to move up to a 9-weight or even 10-weight outfit. Leader breaking strength would also increase to 15- or possibly 20-pound test. This would be taking this aspect of fly fishing to the limit, but the equipment is available for anglers to do it.

FLIES

For our usage, we will define a fly as "a hook with various natural and synthetic materials attached to make a fish strike it." The fish may view the fly as live prey or may hit out of aggression or anger. We don't really care as long as the fish grabs the fly—that is our ultimate goal.

Both subsurface and floating patterns will be reviewed, as fly fishing for bass and panfish has evolved well beyond the use of simple surface poppers, although these designs still catch their share of fish. As mentioned in the introduction, the concept of pattern "templates" will be discussed and presented. These form the building blocks of our basic pattern designs and are often quite simplistic. I was introduced to this idea of fly creation by Kevin Feenstra, an innovative tyer and guide from western Michigan.

I will start with several category templates for subsurface patterns. These types of flies are often overlooked by many fly anglers when targeting bass and panfish, even though the majority of these species' feeding activity is subsurface. Knowing how to both tie and fish these patterns is essential for consistent angling success. From there, we will look at several styles of surface patterns. This gives us a "bottom to top" approach for these fish and the ability to work all parts of the water column—bottom, mid-depth, and surface.

By making adjustments to hook length or adding weight, a basic pattern design can change significantly. Altering materials can do the same. The key characteristics from one template can be combined with the same from another to create a successful pattern. New materials come onto the scene regularly that may improve an existing design.

All these patterns can be tied in both realistic and attractor versions. Realistic patterns are meant to simulate living organisms, be they baitfish, crayfish, leech, frog, or mouse, while attractors use color, flash, and, at times, sound to entice the fish to strike them. Both styles should be in your fly box. Water conditions and time of year often dictate which type of fly to fish.

Finally, we need to learn to construct flies that are durable and will hold together under both the strain of casting and when taken by a fish. Having a fly fall apart after being cast for five minutes is discouraging. Just a bit of extra effort by the tyer will help construct a fly that is durable and long-lasting.

Chapter 2

Getting Started

Necessary Tools

As with any job, having the right tools makes the fly-tying process simpler, quicker, and more efficient. You should buy the best tools that you can afford. The importance of this statement can't be stressed too much. A set of high-quality tools will last for years and do the jobs they were designed for. For bass and panfish, a basic selection of tools should be as follows:

Vise

This will likely be the single most important piece of tying equipment you purchase. The vise holds the hook. It needs to *firmly* hold a variety of hook sizes so that the hook does not slide or move during the tying procedure. The vise should also be easily adjustable to hold the different-size hooks that you will use.

There are many different styles of fly-tying vises on the market these days. If planning to just tie occasionally, a simple lever/cam design may suffice.

This simple cam/lever-design vise clamps to the tying table and has a fixed-angle head. It works best for medium-size hooks.

This style of vise will hold the range of hook sizes needed for most bass and panfish flies. Given that the lower-cost models of this style may have difficulty holding larger hooks securely, it makes sense to try a vise with the hook size you plan to use before you make your purchase.

The basic version of this style vise sits at a fixed angle. You may also find them with an adjustable angle so that the collet tube and jaws can be set parallel with the tying surface and allow the jaws to be turned to easily inspect the fly during the tying process. This works for hooks #10 and larger. It is easier to work on smaller hooks with the vise left at an angle. With this style of vise, the thread and materials are wrapped around the hook shank by the tyer.

The Regal Vise Company offers spring-loaded jaws that are opened by squeezing a lever. These hold hooks very securely and allow a wide range of hook sizes to be used without stopping to make adjustments. They tend to weigh more than other brands but provide superb hook-holding strength.

This Regal Vise holds a wide range of hook sizes very securely and excels at gripping larger hooks. The head can be turned to inspect the fly and the angle adjusted for the tyer's comfort and convenience. The pedestal allows it to be used anywhere.

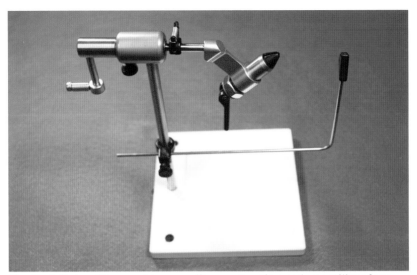

The Peak Rotary Vise combines quality construction and versatility of use at a reasonable price. All features considered, it is one of the best vises on the market.

Another popular style of vise is the rotary design. In this type of vise, the hook shank rotates on a center axis while the tyer turns a crank arm. This design allows for a full, 360-degree view of the fly while it's being tied and precise placement of any materials that are being wrapped. Instead of wrapping materials around the hook, the hook itself is turned while materials are guided down the hook shank.

The rotary vise also has an arm that holds the thread and bobbin stationary while the hook is rotated. Most tyers invariably end up getting a rotary vise as their skills develop and needs expand. I would suggest that if you are at all serious about tying, get a rotary vise right from the start. Top brands in rotary vises are Dyna-King, Peak, and Renzetti.

Most vises are available with either a C-clamp or a pedestal mounting system. The C-clamp is lighter weight and requires an overhang of the tying surface for attachment. If the overhang is thicker than the adjustment range of the clamp, the vise can't be mounted. The pedestal design is, by far, the most popular and can be used on any flat surface.

The C-clamp does provide a greater range of height adjustment, so consider the height of your tying surface if you go with the pedestal vise. You need to be able to reach the hook comfortably without having to extend your arms too far out or up, putting extra strain on your upper arms and shoulders.

A variety of accessories can be added to the vise to make tying easier and more productive. Most vises come with a material holder that works to separate tying materials and keep them from tangling. There are plates that attach to the vise shaft and provide a fixed background color and eliminate glare, along with lights designed to attach to the vise shaft and ensure proper lighting regardless of where you tie.

As mentioned earlier, you should try several styles and brands of vises before purchasing one. Make sure that the vise "fits you," meaning it will perform the functions that you need. It is often better to grow into a vise than to find out the one you have is not adequate for your needs. A quality vise is a precision tool, designed to last a lifetime and beyond.

Scissors

As a key component of your fly-tying equipment, your scissors need to be sharp and stay sharp through constant use. For bass and panfish flies, you really need two pairs of scissors. A pair with a fine point is needed for trimming materials and thread close to the hook. The second pair should be larger and sturdier for cutting heavier materials and working with the various hair types.

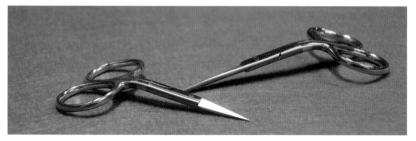

Quality scissors are a must for fly tying. Dr. Slick's Bent Shaft Scissors are one of the top designs.

Some tyers prefer to keep the scissors in their wrapping hand at all times. In this case, the finger holes on the scissors need to be large enough for the scissors to be held even while allowing for ample manipulation. The blades need to be long enough to extend past your palm to avoid cutting or stabbing yourself. Again, you should try scissors before purchasing to make sure they are comfortable in your hand.

I believe the Bent Shaft Scissors from Dr. Slick to be the best on the market for the widest range of fly-tying applications. The 3½-inch size works well for fine close-up work, and the 4½-inch size will cut just about anything. The finger holes are large, and the bend in the shaft allows them to fit comfortably in your palm. They are easily picked up from the tying surface and can be turned at a variety of angles for cutting and trimming.

Bobbin

The bobbin is used to hold thread during the tying process. It helps maintain tension on the thread, allows the tyer to place the thread wraps precisely, and eliminates the need the touch the thread. The most popular bobbins hold the thread spool between two spring arms. These arms can be bent to adjust the pressure holding the spool. There should be enough tension to keep the thread from unrolling off the spool when

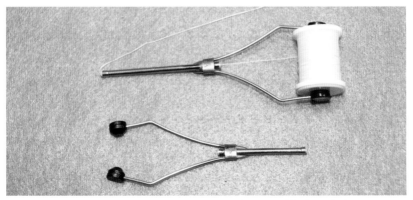

The bobbin holds thread securely and helps the tyer with thread placement when wrapping. The ones pictured here have ceramic inserts in the tube to stop thread wear.

it is hanging, but not so much that it is difficult to roll or feed the thread out when wrapping.

Pay close attention to the bobbin tube, especially when tying larger flies. The larger thread used, and the increased tension on the thread, can wear a cut or groove in the tube, causing the thread to fray and break. It generally takes a period of extended use for this to happen with a quality bobbin. Bobbins are also available with ceramic inserts, which eliminate any chance of thread cutting the tube. The upfront cost is a bit more, but these bobbins will last several lifetimes.

Thread tubes are available in different lengths. I prefer a longer rather than a shorter tube, as it allows better placement of the thread. Try several bobbins out to see which is more comfortable in your hand. Also, put a spool of thread in to check tension and make sure that it is adjustable.

Finally, as I work, I like to have several bobbins loaded and ready to tie. If you happen to break the thread while tying, you will have a bobbin ready to restart the thread and finish the fly without having to rethread the bobbin right away.

Hackle Pliers

In fly-tying terminology, a feather that is wrapped around a hook is called a hackle. Hackle pliers are designed to grip the feathers firmly while they're being wrapped. The hackle pliers also perform tasks such as holding loose threads or ends of other materials. The spring-loaded jaws push apart to grab the feather tip. Avoid small-size pliers, as they are difficult to operate.

Make sure the hackle pliers you use are comfortable in hand

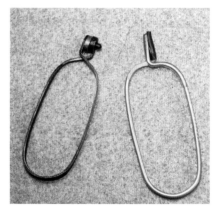

Hackle pliers allow tyers to grip feathers. Rubber pads on the jaws hold better and reduce breakage of fragile feathers. Larger sizes are easier to work with.

and will grip without the feather slipping or being cut. Surgical tubing or shrink-wrap can be put on one jaw to improve the grip. Sharp edges or burrs on the jaws can be removed by polishing with extra-fine steel wool or emery cloth.

Bodkin/Half-Hitch Tool

This combo tool serves several purposes. First, the needle end is used to separate material fibers, pick out fibers tied down by mistake, apply head cement to thread, and open up hook eyes sealed by cement. It is also referred to as a dubbing needle, as it can be used to pick out dubbing furs.

The tapered, hollow end of the tool is slid over the hook eye and used to create a half-hitch knot that slides off the tapered end behind the hook. This knot keeps the thread from unwrapping and is the simplest knot there is to finish the head of the fly. Several half-hitch knots can be done in a series, adding security, and then covered with head cement, clear nail polish, or superglue.

It is also possible to put in half-hitch knots by hand, although placement of the knot is more difficult when doing it by hand, and any dry skin on your fingers may fray the thread. Any hollow tube can be used to make a half-hitch as long as the end of the tube fits over the eye of the hook you are using. In a pinch, a coffee-stirrer straw is very serviceable for larger hooks.

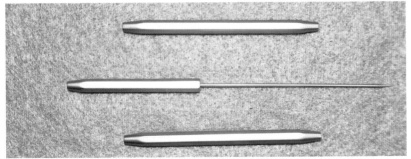

The bodkin needle is used to loosen trapped fibers, pick out furs, and apply cement to thread. The half-hitch tool has a tapered head with different-diameter openings to go over the hook eye when tying off thread.

Other Useful Tools
Bobbin Threader

Many tyers get the thread through the bobbin by starting it at the end of the tube closest to the spool and then sucking the thread through the tube. If this doesn't appeal to you, a bobbin threader will accomplish the task. This is usually a pointed, fine-wire loop mounted on a handle and pushed through the bobbin tube from the top. The tying thread is fed through the wire loop, which is then pulled back through the bobbin tube. Lightweight monofilament line can also be used to do this by doubling it over and pushing it through the bobbin tube.

Whip Finisher

This is used to tie the most effective knot to finish the fly, the whip finish. With this knot the thread is wrapped over itself multiple times to prevent it from unraveling. I finish most flies with two five- or six-wrap whip finish knots. This is extremely secure and durable, and actually eliminates the need to coat the thread with cement or nail polish. The tool takes a bit of practice to master, but will allow you to make the most durable flies

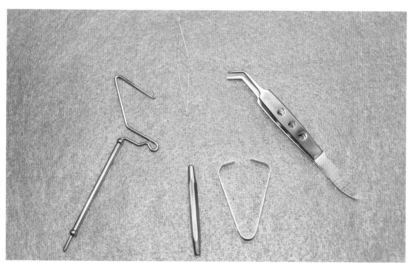

From left to right: whip finisher, bobbin threader, hair packer, and tweezers

possible. I prefer the Materelli style as the easiest to use and learn on. The whip finish knot can also be applied by hand, but in this case, accurate placement and fraying of thread due to dry skin becomes an issue.

Hair Stacker

This tubular metal tool is also referred to as a hair evener. It is very useful when working with bucktail, deer body, and other stiff hairs. Bunches of hair are cut off a hide and put into the metal tube, tips down. The tool is then tapped sharply on a firm surface, causing all the hairs to fall to the bottom of the tube and be evenly aligned. Stackers come in various sizes based on the diameter and length of the hair bunches being used. For our needs, the medium-size to large stackers are best.

The hair-stacking tool is used to even up the ends of stiffer hairs such as deer body hair and bucktail.

Hair Packer

This tool is a big help when spinning deer or similar hair for surface bugs. As each bunch is spun on the hook shank, the hair packer is used to push, or "pack," that bunch as tight as possible against the previous one. This replaces using the nails of our thumb and index finger to pack the hair. The Brassie Hair Packers made by Whitetail Fly Tieing are inexpensive and work great.

Tweezers

These come in handy for assorted tasks such as picking up hooks, beads, and other small items.

Suppliers of top-quality tools include Anvil, Cascade Crest, Dr. Slick, Griffin, Materelli, and Tiemco, among others.

The Tying Area

The fly-tying area can be a permanent location that has a dedicated spot for vise placement, or it might be a temporary spot used only for a few hours. In both cases, there needs to be a flat work area, like a desk or tabletop, with ample room to lay out materials and do the required work. A light-colored background is best for tying. If the work-area surface is too dark, place a sheet or two of blank copy paper behind the vise.

Proper lighting is an absolute necessity to avoid eyestrain. Overhead fluorescent lighting works fine, but is not always available. There are various lights on the market that emit a natural light spectrum showing materials in their true colors. The newest versions have LED elements that stay cool and do not make the tying area uncomfortably warm or burn you if the light housing is touched or bumped. My favorite lights include the Peak Fly Tyers LED Lamp, which attaches to the vise shaft, and the freestanding Pro-Lite from Alert Stamping. The Pro-Lite comes in two styles—one with a double light and the other with a light and a magnifying lens.

The author's tying area is well lit, with plenty of room to move around and reach materials. It is rarely this clean and neat.

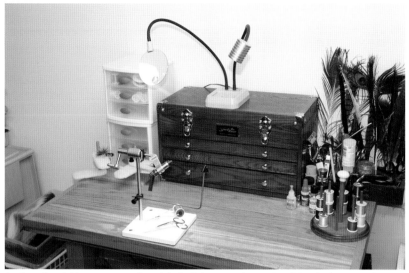

A vise should be at a comfortable height to reduce shoulder fatigue. A light-colored tying background is best, and supplemental light should be used, if needed, to reduce eyestrain.

MATERIALS

The materials used in fly tying come from a wide range of sources. New materials are constantly coming on the market. And while it's well beyond the scope of this work to try to present the full range of natural and synthetic materials available, I'll highlight the items I use for the patterns and variations listed. Keep in mind that in some cases there may be other materials that could be incorporated into the pattern template to create additional fly designs. Such is the joy of fly tying—the creative process is never ending.

One of the current trends in many tying materials is the incorporation of ultraviolet (UV) light-enhancing fibers and other ingredients to create better fish-attracting patterns. Keep in mind that UV materials require direct sunlight in order to work effectively. If it is cloudy, or early or late in the day, the effectiveness of any UV materials will be reduced.

Hooks

There are many brands of hooks on the market, in dozens of styles and sizes. In an effort to keep things simple, I will give the hooks I normally use for specific applications.

As with tools, use the highest-quality hooks you can afford. The chemically sharpened hooks on the market have needle-sharp points, small barbs, and consistent quality. They cost a few cents more than standard hooks, but will result in bringing more fish to hand over the course of time. Several well-recognized names in top-quality fly-tying hooks are Daiichi, Gamakatsu, Mustad Signature Series, and Tiemco.

The hooks we will use include the Daiichi 2460 or 2461 for standard baitfish imitations, plus the Daiichi 1710 and 1760 for crayfish and stand-up-style patterns. The Daiichi 4630, brought in from the conventional bass market, gives a different twist on subsurface patterns.

The Tiemco 8089 is likely the best recognized surface bug and popper hook on the market. It has a wide-gap design to reach around

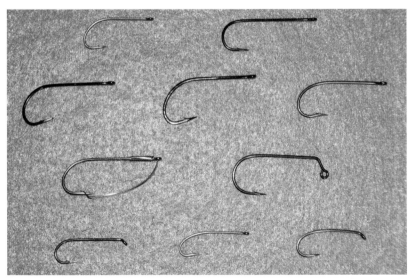

An assortment of hooks for tying bass and panfish flies. From left to right, top row: TMC 8089, Daiichi 2461; second row: Mustad Signature C52SBLN, Gamakatsu B10S, Mustad 3366; third row: Gamakatsu Wire Guard Worm Hook, Daiichi 4630; bottom row: Daiichi 1710, Tiemco (TMC) 200R, Daiichi 1760.

heavy-boned bass jaws, and its light wire aids in flotation. The Tiemco 200R can serve many purposes, including baitfish, rubber spiders, and nymphs. It is available in a wide range of sizes.

The Gamakatsu B10S has come onto the scene in recent years. It makes for great bugs as well as baitfish patterns, and may be the most versatile of hooks on the market. This is another wide-gap design that is strong, needle sharp, and has a full range of sizes to cover everything but the smallest panfish patterns. It is pricey, but practical. The Mustad Signature Series C52SBLN is similar to the B10S, but with a longer shank.

If your budget restricts hook purchasing, opt for the standard Mustad 3366. This hook serves well for most of the patterns we will look at and comes in at a reduced cost. It lacks the overall quality and characteristics of higher priced hooks, but is still functional.

Weedless hooks are certainly a help when fishing in heavy cover, and you can make most patterns weedless by tying in a monofilament guard. This does take a bit of time and effort, so an alternative would be to use hooks with a weed guard already installed. Here I like the Gamakatsu Wire Guard Worm Hook. With a light wire weed guard built into it, it's available in sizes conducive to our needs. This hook is expensive but will save time and, if the fly is well made, be usable for a long time.

A final word about hooks: There are no standards regarding sizing, length, hook strength, etc., that manufacturers are required to follow. As a result, these can vary considerably between manufacturers, creating considerable confusion. The models given above are not the only hooks that can be used, as similar styles may be available from multiple manufacturers.

Thread

Selecting which thread to use is a never-ending source of confusion for beginners. There are many brands of thread on the market, with each brand having its own size scale. In order to simplify things, I am going

UTC thread comes in several thicknesses, or deniers. It is strong, ties flat, and comes in a wide assortment of colors.

to reference only one thread brand, UTC, which I use for nearly all of my tying. This thread is nylon with a bit of stretch to it, and lays flat when wrapped. It is quite strong for the diameter and comes in an extensive range of colors.

I use UTC 70 Denier for hooks #8 and smaller. For hooks #6 to #2/0, I generally use UTC 140 Denier. For hooks larger than #2/0 and doing extensive spinning of deer and similar hair, I would switch to 210 Denier. I find the 140 Denier to be extremely versatile and strong enough to do a lot of the deer-hair work I need. I do not personally tie many intricate hair bugs, hence my use of even 210 Denier is limited.

Body Materials

These are the various products and materials that can be wrapped around the shank of the hook. We will show standard chenille and several other versions to illustrate how a simple change in body material on a pattern template can give an entirely different look to the fly. There are numerous chenille-type materials presently available to tyers. By making very simple body material substitutions, variations of patterns can be easily created.

The eyed tail feather of a peacock is used to make a body that can be particularly effective on smaller bluegill patterns. The individual fibers off the tail, called "herl," are wrapped on the hook shank. The natural iridescence of this material has made it a favorite of fly tyers for several centuries.

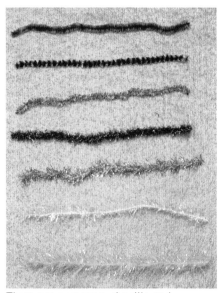

There are numerous chenille and chenille-like materials that can be used as body materials. From top to bottom: standard chenille, variegated chenille, New Age Chenille, sparkle chenille, metallic tinsel chenille, Estaz, Cactus Chenille.

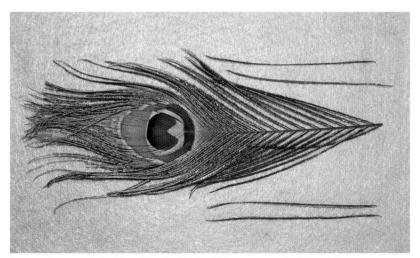

An eyed peacock feather. The individual fibers are called "herl."

Feathers

Most of the feathers used for fly-tying applications come from gallina-ceous, ground-dwelling birds like chickens, pheasants, or other game birds, as well as a variety of waterfowl. As mentioned, hackles are feath-ers that are wrapped around the hook. Different types of hackles come from different parts of the bird's body. They come in a wide range of natural colors and can also be dyed nearly any color imaginable.

Bass and panfish flies require different types of feathers. Shown here, the top two feathers are saddle hackles, the middle two are neck hackles, and the bottom two are marabou plumes.

For our applications, we will use both neck and saddle hackles from chickens. Saddle hackles are long, thin feathers that can be easily wrapped around the hook shank to give bulk to the fly, as well as the appearance of legs. The neck hackles we use have a stiffer center shaft and simulate kicking legs on surface patterns. These can be purchased on the skin, or pelt, of a bird or sorted and bagged.

Marabou will be used for tails. These are soft under-feathers from the body of a turkey. They compress when wet and undulate as the fly is retrieved. Marabou is also dyed many different colors, along with assorted color combinations.

Tails, Hairs, and Furs

Various animal tails can be incorporated into a wide range of patterns. Bucktail comes from whitetail deer and provides a long, straight hair useful for baitfish imitations. It comes in both natural and dyed colors. Tip-dyed bucktails are now available that add another color dimension

Bucktail is a key component in tying the Clouser Deep Minnow. It is available in dyed and natural colors, and in whole tails or pieces.

Squirrel tail (top) and arctic fox tail (bottom) can be incorporated into many bass and panfish flies.

to baitfish patterns. Squirrel tail can also be incorporated into a number of bass and panfish patterns. Red and fox squirrel make very realistic pincers on crayfish patterns.

Normally used for salmon and steelhead patterns, arctic fox tail, with its durability and great movement in the water, can also be used as a substitute for both marabou and bucktail. Again, natural and dyed colors are available.

Deer body hair is used extensively in the construction of surface poppers and divers. This is different from bucktail, being that it is shorter, coarser, and partly hollow. Hair from

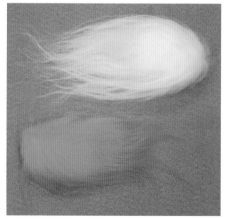

Icelandic sheep hair is long, durable, and has great movement in the water. It compresses when wet and does not pick up water weight, making it a good material for larger patterns.

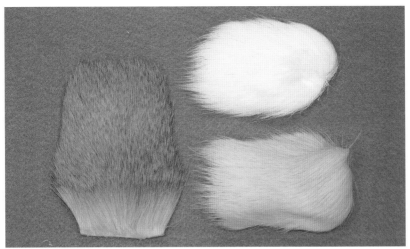

Deer body hair (left) and belly hair (right) are used to make intricate and artful divers and poppers for bass and panfish.

both the belly and back of the animal is used. Belly hair is pure white and gives much brighter colors when dyed. Hair from the back and sides is a gray-brown color and does not show dyed color as well.

Icelandic sheep body hair can be used to construct diving patterns for bass. This hair gives length and bulk to the fly with plenty of movement. The beauty of this material is its durability and how it compresses to almost nothing when out of the water, making it much easier to cast.

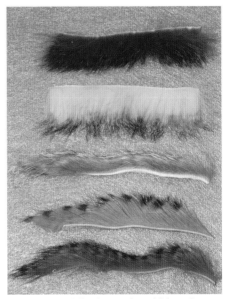

Crosscut and Zonker-style rabbit strips are found in a wide range of natural and dyed colors. They are very durable, with great movement in the water.

Rabbit fur has been a staple fly-tying material for decades. It is very durable, with great movement. When left on the hide, it can be cut following the direction of the hair and called simply a strip. When the cut is perpendicular to the hair, it is referred to as crosscut. Strips can be used to make backs, tails, and crayfish pincers. Crosscut strips are wrapped around the hook like a hackle. The same fur cut different ways gives totally different looks. There are many natural and dyed color variations.

Synthetic Hair and Flash

I am not a big proponent of synthetic hairs on most bass and panfish flies. The exception to this would be Extra Select Craft Fur, which serves as both a bucktail and marabou substitute and is available in a multitude of colors. It can be used alone or in combination with other materials.

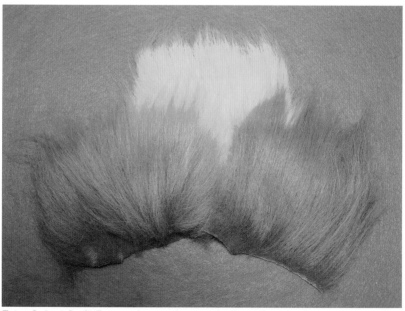

Extra Select Craft Fur can be used as a substitute for marabou and bucktail on smaller streamer patterns.

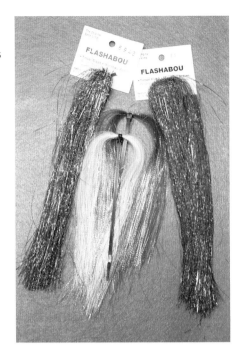

Krinkle Mirror Flash (middle) has a great minnow-like look in the water. Holographic Flashabou has color, flash, and great movement.

There are many different types of flash materials available to fly tyers. I use two most often: Holographic Flashabou is available in both solid and blended colors, and works best to accent and brighten combinations of color. A bit harder to find, Cascade Crest's Krinkle Mirror Flash makes baitfish patterns appear as realistic as possible. This material mimics the sides of turning or flashing baitfish.

Eyes, Heads, Weight, and Legs

Hollow plastic doll eyes are often incorporated into surface patterns for bass. They may add some buoyancy and a bit of noise when the pupils rattle, but I am not convinced that they are worth the effort required to attach them securely to the fly. They enhance the appearance of the fly to the angler, but I'm not sure how much they help in catching fish.

There are several styles of cast and machined eyes available to the tyer. They are generally cast lead or machined brass. Some are painted

An extensive selection of barbell-style weighted eyes are available in a wide range of shapes, sizes, and colors.

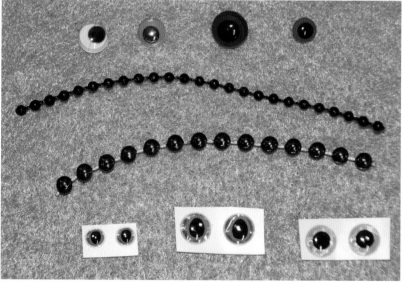

Various glue-on, stick-on, and plastic bead-chain eyes can be incorporated into different fly patterns.

to look like eyes, while others have stick-on eyes that can be attached to them. These provide weight to help sink the fly and give a more realistic appearance to baitfish patterns. In this application, using them for baitfish imitations, I believe eyes do increase the effectiveness of the fly. The weight of the eye and its placement on the hook shank can influence how the fly swims. They are usually attached on the top of the shank so that the hook rides inverted.

Bead chain is available in both metal and plastic and can be incorporated into smaller patterns for panfish. Plastic bead chain makes realistic eyes for crayfish and dragonfly nymph patterns. Metal bead chain adds a small bit of weight and, in black, can also serve as eyes.

Various metal cones and larger beads can be used to weight the front of many patterns, helping them sink and adding a bit of flash. A recent advancement in this style of weight, the Fish-Skull from Flymen Fishing Company gives a more realistic profile of a baitfish head with eyes. The Sculpin Helmet from the same company provides the profile of a number of bottom-dwelling critters such as sculpin and gobies.

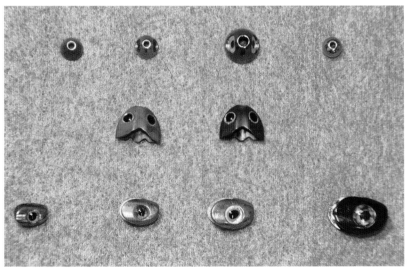

Weighted beads, cones, and heads can be added to bass and panfish patterns. The Sculpin Helmet (middle row) and Fish-Skull are among the most recently developed of these types of product.

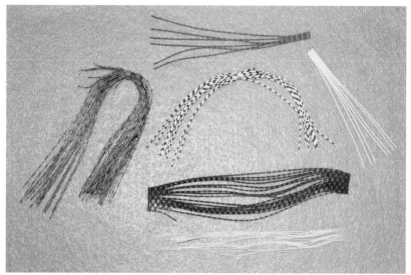

Rubber legs and rubber hackle can be added to many patterns to increase their effectiveness.

Of course, lead wire or a nontoxic substitute can also be wrapped on the hook shank to weight the fly. Placement of the wire on the body can affect how the fly sinks and swims. For easy wrapping, use wire of a diameter similar to that of the hook shank or slightly smaller.

A variety of rubber legs, when added to bass and panfish flies, enhance both the action and the appearance of the fly. This is often referred to as "rubber hackle" and for years was only available in solid colors. We now have versions in both flat and round shape in a multitude of color combinations, including solid, barred, speckled, and metallic.

Foam

Several styles of closed-cell foam can be used to create effective, durable, and easy-to-tie floating patterns for bass and panfish. These styles come as preformed bodies as well as sheets of foam wherein a strip is cut off or a desired shape is cut out of a sheet. There are also foam cylinders available in different diameters that can be cut to a desired length.

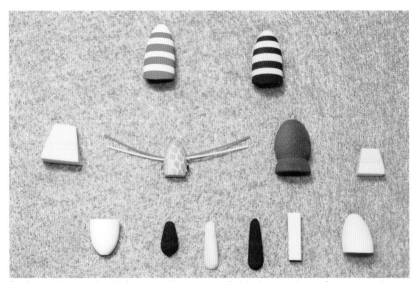

Preformed closed-cell foam bodies are available in a variety of shapes, sizes, and colors. Their use simplifies the process of making a number of surface patterns.

The simplest of these are ant and spider bodies in different sizes and colors. Wrapped onto a hook, a bit of feather or rubber hackle completes the fly. With larger preformed bodies, a shallow cut is normally made in the bottom and the hook is glued into the cut. Some will also have a predrilled hole in the body wherein the hook shank is inserted and glued.

Many preformed bodies are flat on one end and tapered on the other. These can be made into a popper by positioning the flat end forward or made into a slider by placing the tapered end forward. Blockhead foam can be either a popper or diver, depending on which end of the body is put forward. Some of these bodies will also have rubber legs already attached to them, simplifying the tying process even more.

Chapter 3

Basic Techniques

STARTING THE THREAD

1. Seat the thread spool in the bobbin and pull thread through the tube.

2. Place the hook in the vise so that the shank is parallel to the tying surface. The hook point should extend slightly past the jaws; this allows access to the start of the bend.

3. If you are right-handed, with about 6 inches of thread out of the bobbin, hold the thread in your left hand. With your right hand, grip the bobbin at the bottom of the tube.

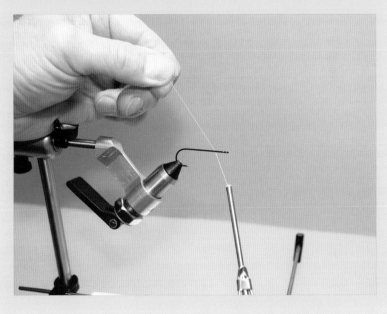

4. Move your left hand with the thread behind the hook shank, the right hand with the bobbin below the shank. Keeping tension on the thread at an angle, wrap the thread in your right hand away from you and back over the thread in your left hand several times. This locks the thread in, and the bobbin can now be left to hang.

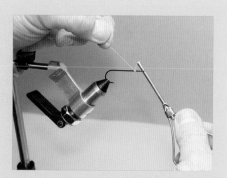

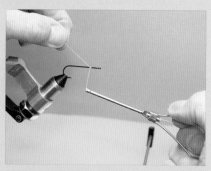

5. With scissors, trim the loose end of the thread (also called the tag end) as close to the shank as possible.

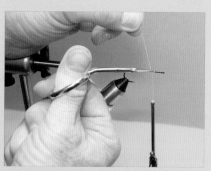

Thread started and locked in

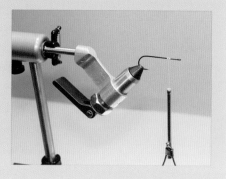

Wrapping the Thread

Covering the shank with thread, note that the bend of the hook starts at a point between the barb and point of the hook.

1. Wrap the thread away from you under tension.

2. You'll notice that the length of thread out of the bobbin gets shorter as you wrap. Tension on the bobbin may be light enough that you can continue to wrap and thread will feed out. If not, use your thumb and index finger to roll out thread, a little at a time, as you are wrapping.

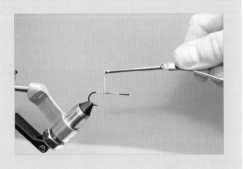

Practice starting, wrapping, and finishing off the thread a number of times until you are comfortable and proficient with the procedure. Try to keep 2 to 3 inches of thread from the bobbin to the hook shank when wrapping. This allows accurate placement of the thread and enables you to see other parts of the fly clearly.

FINISHING OFF THE THREAD

1. With the thread up to the eye of the hook, pick up a half-hitch tool with your right hand, making sure that the open end of the tool will fit over the hook eye.

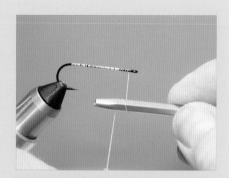

2. Grab the thread bobbin in your left hand, extend 4 to 6 inches of thread out of the bobbin, and lay the half-hitch tool on the thread. Keeping tension, wrap the thread around the half-hitch tool to the left side of the thread, coming down from the hook eye.

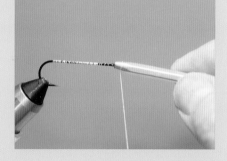

3. Slide the open end of the half-hitch tool over the hook eye.

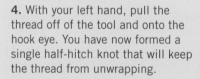

4. With your left hand, pull the thread off of the tool and onto the hook eye. You have now formed a single half-hitch knot that will keep the thread from unwrapping.

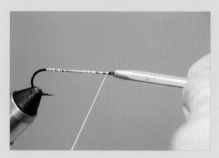

5. Repeat this procedure several times, making a series of half-hitch knots at the hook eye.

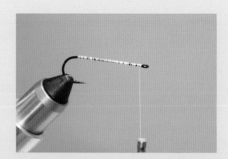

6. With light tension, trim the thread as close to the hook shank as possible, then coat with head cement or a touch of superglue.

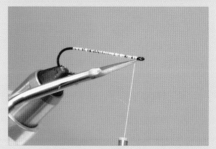

Note: You can make double wraps of thread when forming the half-hitch knot, but it will create a bit more bulk. It is also possible to do the half-hitch by hand, but is easier and more convenient to do it with a tool. Finally, the ultimate wrap knot is called the whip finish. It is a continuous series of wraps of the thread back over itself. We will examine this knot later.

WEIGHTING A BODY

Note: Weighting the forward section of the fly will counterbalance the hook bend and make it sink level or slightly downward. If the weight is put too far back, the fly will sink backwards.

1. Start the thread at a point halfway down the hook shank.

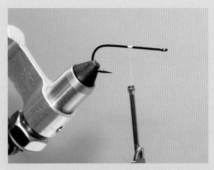

2. Select a lead or non-lead wire substitute, approximately the same diameter as the hook shank.

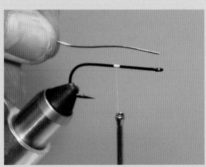

3. Start the wire in front of the thread.

4. Wrap forward toward the eye—leave enough space behind the hook eye to finish the fly.

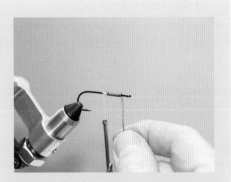

5. The soft wire can be cut with scissors.

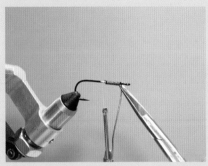

6. Wrap thread back and forth over the wire several times to secure it in place, then wrap back to the bend of the hook and begin the fly.

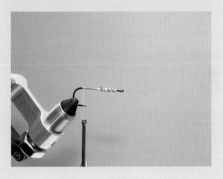

Tying in Barbell Eyes

The size of the eyes and position on the hook shank determine how much jigging motion the fly will have. For example, the closer to the eye of the hook and heavier the dumbbell eyes, the more up-and-down movement to the fly. Conversely, lighter eyes and those placed more toward the center of the shank will have less movement.

Barbell eyes will also be added as a final step to the fly in some patterns. In this case, the barbell eyes would be tied on just behind the hook eye per steps 2 to 6.

1. Start the thread about one-third of the way down the hook shank from the eye. Keep the thread in a narrow band.

2. Lay the narrow part of the barbell eyes on top of the hook shank at an angle back toward the bend, and make 3 tight wraps of thread. This should secure the eyes on the shank.

3. Adjust the barbell eyes so that it is perpendicular to the hook. Make 3 more wraps around the middle of the eyes. The wraps should now be in an X shape.

4. Do one more set of alternate wraps, then make several tight, circular wraps under the barbell eyes, but over the hook shank, to make the X wraps as tight as possible.

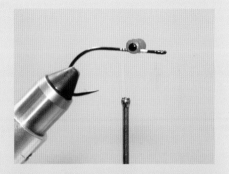

5. Turn the hook over and make sure that the eyes are straight. Put several drops of superglue on the top of the X wraps.

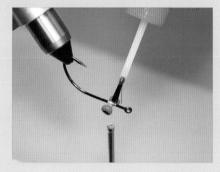

Making a Hook Weedless

1. With the hook in the vise, start the thread at a point halfway down the shank. Lay a base of thread back to a point on the shank opposite the point.

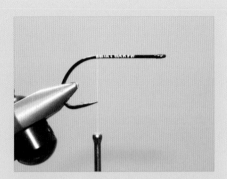

2. Cut a length of stiff 20-pound mono 4 to 5 inches long.

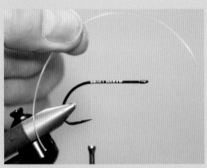

3. Lay the mono along the shank facing you. Wrap the thread over the mono, back to a point halfway around the bend of the hook and then back forward. You can coat the thread at this point and let it dry. Begin tying the fly at this point.

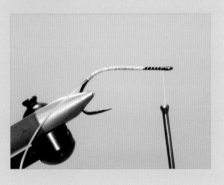

4. After the fly is tied, run the mono up through the hook eye, and make a few thread wraps to lock the mono in place. The mono should be in line from just past the hook point to the eye.

5. Tie the mono down over the eye.

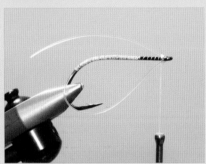

6. Trim the tag end of the mono, wrap the head of the fly, then finish. Coat the head to hold thread and mono in place.

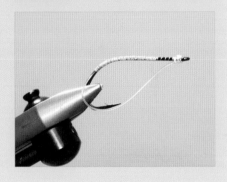

Making the Whip Finish

Note: This is the most secure way to tie off the thread at the end of the tying procedure. Two sets of five-turn whip finishes will hold a fly together under almost any conditions. Learning this technique is needed in order to tie off the thread behind beads, cones, and popper bodies.

1. With your left hand holding the bobbin, pull off about 5 inches of thread. Holding the whip finisher in your right hand, place the hooked end of the bobbin onto the thread.

2. Wrap the thread around the notch in the bobbin wire, and pull the thread up to where it comes off the shank. This forms a triangle.

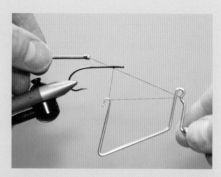

3. Holding the whip finisher, flip the triangle over and let the finisher rotate as you wrap the finisher in a circular motion. Make sure the thread locks behind the hook eye.

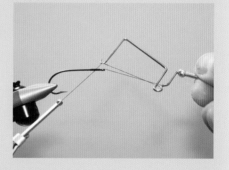

4. The thread coming off of the hooked end will wrap around the thread coming off the notch. Wrap the thread behind the hook eye 5 or 6 times.

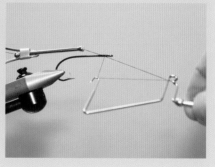

5. Keeping tension on the thread, tilt the finisher so that the thread slides out of the notch. The thread will stay in the hooked end of the finisher.

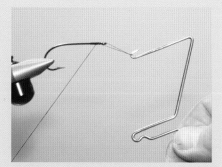

6. Pull with your left hand so that the loop of thread in the hooked end is pulled under the wrapped thread.

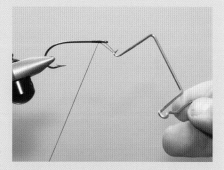

7. Let the thread slide off the hooked end of the finisher, then pull the thread tight and trim.

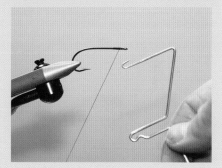

Chapter 4

Below the Surface

As mentioned earlier, subsurface patterns can imitate many different life forms, including baitfish, insect larvae, crayfish, and frogs. They can be realistic—made to look like a specific organism—or just a combination of flash and movement to tempt a fish into striking. After a simplistic introductory pattern, we will examine two main pattern templates, the Woolly Bugger and Deep Minnow. These can be altered to suggest a wide range of food items that bass or panfish are likely to encounter.

Note: As we review the following patterns and variations, there will be material substitutions and additions as we progress to illustrate how various components can be incorporated into a pattern template and create different looks. A reminder: *All instructions and photos are based on tying right-handed*.

The Sinking Spider

This simple pattern shows us how to wrap a body and add rubber legs to the fly. It works well for bluegill, sunfish, and crappie, but don't be surprised when a sizable largemouth grabs one. The main color schemes are black, chartreuse, or a white body with contrasting color legs.

Hook: Daiichi 1710, #8 to #12
Thread: UTC 70 Denier
Body: Chenille
Legs: Fine or micro round rubber legs

1. Start the thread and wrap a base over the hook shank. Take the thread back to a point between the point and the barb.

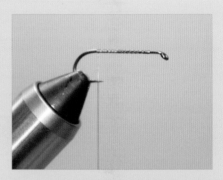

2. Take a length of chenille about 4 inches long and hold it in your left hand. With your right thumb and index finger, strip a bit of the "fuzzy" materials off the thread core.

3. Hold the exposed thread core of the chenille right where the thread stops on the hook with your left hand. Take the bobbin in your left hand and wrap the thread over the core material of the chenille. Make several extra secure wraps of thread and then advance the thread toward the hook eye, leaving some space to the hook eye.

4. Wrap the chenille away from you over the hook shank, keeping each wrap tight and directly in front of the previous wrap.

5. When you reach the thread, hold the chenille in front of the thread and make several tight wraps over the top of the chenille, securing it.

6. Trim the excess chenille, making sure not to cut the thread in the process.

7. Cut a 2- to 3-inch length of the round rubber hackle.

8. Fold the rubber hackle in half and tie in where it is folded. Try to catch the tip of the folded hackle, then give several thread wraps to secure. Repeat the process on the other side of the fly.

9. Trim any excess materials as close as you can and form a neat, tapered head with your thread.

10. Tie off the thread with a series of half-hitch knots or whip finish. Trim the thread as close as you can and coat with a clear cement or a touch of superglue.

THE WOOLLY BUGGER FAMILY

The Woolly Bugger family

The Sinking Spider Variation

A simple variation of this fly would be to tie the legs into the middle of the body. In this case, the chenille is wrapped halfway up the shank, then tied off and trimmed. The legs are tied in, then the chenille is tied in and wrapped

forward, where it is tied off, trimmed, and the thread finished.

Please note: I chose to include the Sinking Spider patterns as part of the Woolly Bugger Family as it shows us how to use and wrap a chenille body—a primary component of the Woolly Bugger pattern.

The Basic Woolly Bugger

Few patterns are as versatile as the Woolly Bugger—it imitates few things exactly, but looks like many things. Hook length, color, and certain materials can be altered to change its look considerably. Weight can be added in several different ways to change how it moves in the water. In fact, it is probably hard to tie this fly so that it will not catch fish. In addition, it is a great starter pattern, as it teaches a number of key tying techniques, including adding a tail, wrapping a body, and winding a hackle. Black, olive, brown, tan, chartreuse, and white are the key color schemes in the pattern.

Hook: Daiichi 2461 (or any suitable streamer hook), #1/0 to #10
Thread: UTC 140 or 70 Denier, depending on hook size
Tail: Marabou
Body: Chenille
Hackle: Saddle hackle

1. Start the thread and wrap a base, then take the thread back to a point between the hook point and barb.

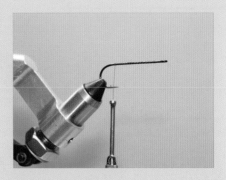

2. Select a marabou plume, hold it by the tip, and peel away the lower part of the feather.

3. Measure the length of the plume to tie in as approximately the length of the hook shank. Pinch the feather at this point.

4. Move the marabou plume back to right (the point) where the thread is hanging. Hold the marabou on top of the hook shank with your left hand, and with your right hand take the thread over the top of the marabou. Make 3 or 4 wraps to secure the marabou in place. If the marabou wants to roll off the hook shank, reduce tension on the thread, then take the thread over the marabou and pull straight down with firm pressure. When the marabou is secure, trim the excess material sticking out to the front as close as possible to the shank of the hook.

5. Prepare a saddle hackle by cutting off the tip point and then trimming 5 or 6 hackle barbules on each side of the center shaft of the feather. Secure the feather, right on top of the tail, by wrapping thread over the trimmed hackle barbules. Do not advance the thread forward up the hook shank.

6. Tie in a 5- to 6-inch length of chenille on top of the tail and hackle by wrapping thread over the exposed center core of the chenille.

7. Advance the thread forward, leaving space behind the hook eye to tie off materials and finish the head of the fly. ***This step is very important.*** Most beginners tend to crowd the hook eye and run out of room. Leave more room than you think you will need.

8. Wrap the chenille forward, making sure that each wrap is directly in front of the other. Keep the body smooth, with no gaps or spaces.

9. When you get close to the eye, tie off and trim the chenille. Be careful not to cut both the chenille and the thread. You can hold the chenille with the left thumb and index finger while you push the thread back out of the way with the other fingers on the right hand while cutting with your scissors in the right hand.

10. Grasp the loose end of the saddle hackle by squeezing the hackle pliers to open them and then releasing to grip the feather.

Wrap the feather forward, over the top of the chenille. Keep the wraps evenly spaced down the hook shank.

11. When you get to the hook eye, tie off the feather and trim the excess as close as you can to the hook shank.

12. With your left thumb and index finger, pull back any feather fibers and wrap a neat, tapered head. Tie off the thread with a series of half hitches, then coat with cement or superglue.

Note: It is important to pay attention to the sequence in which body materials are tied in and then wrapped. In this case, the saddle hackle was tied in first, but wrapped forward last. The chenille was tied in last, but wrapped forward first. This is a critical concept to understand as you advance in fly tying.

The Better Bugger Variation

A drawback of the Woolly Bugger is that it tends to come apart rather easily. Marabou is quite fragile and can break while unhooking a fish. Saddle hackle often breaks and will unravel, making the fly unusable. There are several ways to make the pattern longer lasting and stronger. These are reflected in the Better Bugger.

Hook: Daiichi 2461, #1/0 to #10
Tail: Arctic fox tail
Body: Sparkle chenille with saddle hackle twisted in

Step 1. Start with a wire-weighted hook, prepared as described earlier in the weighting the body (pg. 47).

Steps 2 & 3. In place of marabou, substitute arctic fox tail. This hair has an action very similar to marabou in the water, but is much more durable. Fox tails are cut into cross sections called "medallions." Trim a section of hair around 1/4 inch in diameter from the tail, right at the hide. Holding the hair by the tips, pull out most of the loose hair from down near the hide. Gauge the length of hair to tie in as with marabou—approximately the length of the hook shank.

Step 4. Tie in the tail hair, tips to the rear. Trim away any excess sticking out forward. Then prepare and tie in chenille and a saddle hackle as in the standard Woolly Bugger.

Step 5. Take your hackle pliers and grasp the end of the chenille and the saddle hackle together. Twist the chenille and hackle clockwise several times and then make a wrap over the hook shank to begin forming the body.

Steps 6-7. With each wrap forward, continue to twist the hackle and chenille clockwise. Fill the hook shank up to the eye and then tie off the body and trim away excess. Form a neat thread head, then finish off. By using the arctic fox as the tail and twisting the chenille and saddle together before wrapping the body, the durability of the fly is improved significantly.

Better Bugger Variation (step 1)

Better Bugger Variation (steps 2–3)

Better Bugger Variation (step 4)

Better Bugger Variation (step 5)

Better Bugger Variation (steps 6–7)

The Damsel/Dragon Variation

Aquatic insects represent a primary food source for both bass and panfish. By working with the Woolly Bugger template, minor changes allow us to create a pattern imitating damselflies and dragonflies. These insects are abundant in ponds, lakes, rivers, and streams and are targeted by both bass and panfish when available.

Hook: Tiemco 200R, #6 to #10
Thread: UTC 70 Denier, olive
Tail: Olive grizzly marabou
Hackle: Olive grizzly saddle, small
Body: 4 peacock herl fibers, twisted together and wrapped
Eyes: Plastic bead chain

The completed Damsel/Dragon Variation

1. Tie in the tail and hackle. Four peacock herl fibers are used to form the body. These are tied in at their tips and the butt ends grasped with hackle pliers.

2. Twist the herl fibers clockwise several times before wrapping. This strengthens them and adds bulk. Do this down the length of the hook.

3. Wrap the hackle forward and tie off. To tie in the eyes, hold a length of plastic bead chain and secure with a crisscross wrap, then cut off leaving two after they are secured.

The Baitfish Bugger Variation

The main change in this Bugger variant is the addition of flash to the tail and the use of Estaz or Cactus Chenille, plastic-like body materials.

The completed Baitfish Bugger

Hook: Daiichi 2461, #2/0 to #4, weighted

Thread: UTC 140 Denier, white

Tail: White, gray, or chartreuse marabou or arctic fox, with pearl Krinkle Mirror Flash

Body: Pearl Estaz or Cactus Chenille

Hackle: White saddle

Note: Flash can be added to any Woolly Bugger variation as desired.

1. A wire-wrapped, weighted hook is used, and a tail of marabou added. Tie down several strands of pearl Krinkle Mirror Flash on top of the tail in the middle. Pull back the Krinkle Mirror Flash and then tie it down and trim.

2. A saddle hackle is tied in. Estaz is prepared as standard chenille and tied in. When the Estaz is wrapped forward, pull back the fibers from the previous wrap before making the next wrap. Cover the shank with Estaz to just behind the eye, tie off, and trim. Wrap the hackle forward, then tie off and trim.

Bead-Head or Cone-Head Variation

Adding a bead head or cone head to a fly adds weight and flash, and gives the fly a more jig-like movement in the water. Cones tend to be heavier than beads and are usually more suited to larger hooks. Both are found in a wide range of colors.

Hook: Tiemco 200R, #4 to #10
Thread: UTC 140 Denier
Bead: Sized to hook
Tail: Marabou or arctic fox tail
Body: Chenille, Estaz, or Cactus Chenille
Hackle: Saddle hackle

The completed Bead-Head Variation

1. The bead or cone is put on the hook prior to the fly being tied. Put the hook point through the small hole in the bead and slide the bead up to the hook eye.

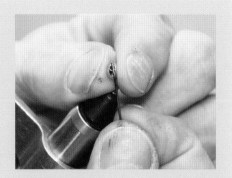

2. Tie in the tail and hackle. Here we also see that a bulkier chenille body can be created by starting the chenille in front, behind the bead, and winding it to the back and then forward again. A double layer of material is put down.

3. Wrap all the materials forward as tight to the bead as possible. The thread needs to be tied off behind the bead. This shows the drawback of using just a half-hitch knot and tool. You need to do this by hand or find a tube large enough to fit over the bead. In this case a straw was used to do a series of half-hitch knots to complete the fly, but illustrates the need to learn to use a whip-finish tool as soon as you pass the beginner stage of tying.

The Hellgrammite Variation

Dobsonfly larvae are also called hellgrammites. They are very common in the faster-moving areas of many smallmouth bass streams, and bass love to eat them. A minor change turns an all-black or dark gray Woolly Bugger into a great hellgrammite imitation. This pattern is

The completed Hellgramite Variation

often dead-drifted under a float or swung across the current. At this point, you should be able to easily tie this pattern having just the recipe and a photo of the finished fly.

Hook: Daiichi 1710, #4
Thread: UTC 140 Denier, black
Tail: Black or dark gray marabou
Body: Black or dark gray chenille
Hackle: Black saddle hackle
Eyes: Small black nickel barbell, tied on behind the eye of the hook after all materials

Simple Crayfish

Crayfish are a primary food source for bass and panfish during the summer months. Many crayfish patterns are complicated to tie and do not fish well. This pattern, a Woolly Bugger offshoot, is simple to master and can be stripped, swung, or fished under a float. It catches fish.

The completed Simple Crayfish

Hook: Daiichi 1710, #4

Thread: UTC 140 Denier, olive

Tail: Olive, brown, or tan marabou, then orange grizzly marabou

Antennae: Rubber hackle

Body: Olive, brown, or tan crosscut rabbit strip, wrapped down shank

Eyes: Small black nickel barbell

1. Tie in the tail and antennae. A 4-inch strip of cross-cut rabbit is held with the fur hanging down. Trim the hair down to the hide and make an angled cut on the right-side end.

2. Tie down the tip of the crosscut strip just in front of the tail, with the fur to the left toward the tail.

3. Wrap the strip forward, with each turn just barely on top of the previous one. Make sure to keep the fur pulled back and clear of the next wrap.

4. Tie off the strip, trim, and form a head.

5. Add a pair of small barbell eyes on the top of the hook shank using the crisscross wrap. This will keep the hook inverted as the fly is being fished. Tie off and finish the head.

Sculpin Bugger

The Sculpin Helmet is a weighted head from Flymen Fishing Company that is slid onto the hook after the fly is tied. It has a wide, flat profile similar to that of a sculpin, goby, or crayfish. This pattern will generally be in an olive, tan, or brown color scheme. The Daiichi 1760 hook marries perfectly to the Sculpin Helmet, creating a stand-up-style pattern to work on the bottom.

Hook: Daiichi 1760, #4
Thread: UTC 140 Denier, olive
Tail: Olive or brown Jailhouse marabou from Spirit River
Body: Olive or root beer Estaz or Cactus Chenille
Hackle: Olive or brown grizzly saddle
Antennae and legs: Cascade Crest Lizard Legs or other rubber hackle
Head: Small or mini Flymen Fishing Company Sculpin Helmet

1. The fly is tied just like a regular Woolly Bugger. Make sure to leave room at the head of the fly to slide on the Sculpin Helmet.

2. Invert the hook with the vise, then coat the front thread and material with superglue and slide on the Sculpin Helmet. Add thread in front of the Sculpin Helmet to secure.

THE DEEP MINNOW FAMILY

The Deep Minnow family

Originally designed for smallmouth bass by Pennsylvania guide Bob Clouser, this pattern has emerged as the single most productive fly for both freshwater and saltwater fly-fishing applications. Called just the Deep Minnow or Clouser Minnow, it is primarily a baitfish imitation, but by varying size, color, and materials, many different looks can be created. It is a simple template that emphasizes the jigging action created by the barbell eyes, and is a must for every fly box.

The Basic Deep Minnow

Hook: Gamakatsu B10S, #2/0 to #8
Thread: UTC 140 or 70 Denier, depending on hook size
Eyes: Barbell style; size varies depending on hook size
Belly: Bucktail
Flash: Krinkle Mirror Flash or Holographic Flashabou
Back: Bucktail

1. Attach the barbell eyes as described in Chapter 3, Basic Techniques, "Tying in Barbell Eyes." Make sure the thread stays behind the eyes.

2. Separate out several dozen fibers from a bucktail and trim them off next to the hide.

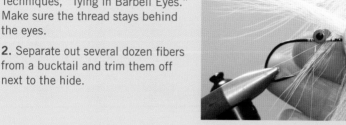

3. Holding the bucktail fibers by the tips in your left hand, pull out any fuzz or short fibers.

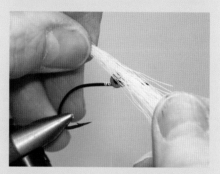

4. Gauge the length of the bucktail approximately twice the length of the shank and tie down securely behind the eyes. If you have trouble with the bucktail rolling off the hook shank as you wrap, reduce tension on the thread and wrap over top of the bucktail, then pull down firmly to secure the bucktail to the hook shank.

5. Pull the butt ends of the bucktail over the narrow part of the eyes and tie down securely, then trim off any excess material extending past the thread.

6. Invert the hook in the vise and cut 5 or 6 strands of Krinkle Mirror Flash from a bunch. Tie the strands down in the middle, then pull back and tie down again to lock them in place. Trim slightly longer than the belly.

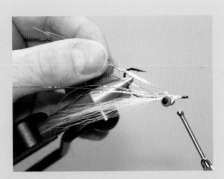

7. Select another bunch of bucktail and prepare, then tie in securely, just like the first. Try to have this bunch be a bit longer than the belly.

8. Trim the excess at different lengths. This allows a smooth tapered head to be formed.

9. Wrap the head and tie off the thread. Coat with cement or superglue.

10. Coat the bucktail pulled over the barbell and the thread behind the eyes to give added strength to the fly.

Note: The chartreuse back/white belly color shown is the most popular for this pattern. Other popular colors are all white, olive/white, gray/white, olive/chartreuse, olive/orange, and brown/orange. Try to keep the amount of bucktail used on the sparse side. This pattern is more effective with less rather than more bucktail.

The completed Basic Deep Minnow

Spottail Shiner Variation

Hook: Gamakatsu B10S, #1
Thread: UTC 140 Denier, olive
Belly: White or cream bucktail
Flash: Pearl Cascade Crest Krinkle Mirror Flash
Back: Olive/black Tip Dyed Bucktail from Spirit River
Eyes: Medium or large barbell style

The Spottail Shiner Variation

Note: This is a great imitation of the spottail shiner, a common bait-fish species across much of the Great Lakes region, the Midwest, and beyond. Overall length should be 3 to 4 inches.

Perch Minnow Variation

Hook: Gamakatsu B10S, #1/0
Thread: UTC 140 Denier, olive
Belly: White or cream bucktail with orange marabou
Flash: Fire tiger Holographic Flashabou
Back: Yellow bucktail with olive bucktail over top; make barred marking with olive or brown permanent marker
Eyes: Large barbell style, gold with black pupil

The Perch Minnow Variation

Jig Deep Minnow

Hook: Daiichi 4630, #2/0
Thread: UTC 140, olive
Tail: Tan arctic fox tail
Belly: White bucktail
Flash: Pearl Cascade Crest Krinkle Mirror Flash
Back: Olive bucktail
Eyes: Large barbell style

The Jig Deep Minnow

Note: The Daiichi 4630 60-degree jig hook makes the fly stay deeper longer on the retrieve. The tail of arctic fox gives additional length to the fly for larger imitations. This pattern can be tied in any baitfish coloration.

Simple Minnow

Hook: TMC 200R, #4
Thread: UTC 140 Denier, olive
Flash: Pearl Cascade Crest Krinkle Mirror Flash
Back: Gray, white, olive, or tan bucktail, with gray squirrel tail over top in front
Eyes: Medium black nickel barbell style

The Simple Minnow

Note: This stripped-down version of the Deep Minnow is quicker and easier to tie. It works well to imitate slender, smaller baitfish.

Crafty Minnow

Hook: Gamakatsu B10S, #4
Thread: UTC 70 Denier, olive
Flash: Pearl Cascade Crest Krinkle Mirror Flash
Back: Olive-gray, chartreuse, white, or olive Extra Select Craft Fur with 2 or 3 peacock herl strands over top
Eye: Small or mini barbell style

The Crafty Minnow

Note: This is another great pattern to imitate fry and smaller baitfish. It is especially effective for crappie and perch.

Fish Head Minnow

Hook: Gamakatsu B10S, #1 to #4

Thread: UTC 140 Denier

Belly: Bucktail or Extra Select Craft Fur

Flash: Pearl Cascade Crest Krinkle Mirror Flash

Back: Bucktail or Extra Select Craft Fur

Head: Flymen Fishing Company Fish Skull, sized to hook, slid on from the front and glued

Note: The Fish Skull is heavier on the bottom and, when put on an inverted hook, will keep the hook riding upright. This pattern can be made in most baitfish colorations.

The Fish Head Minnow

Chapter 5

On the Surface

The willingness of bass and panfish to take flies on the surface has endeared them to fly anglers. The explosive strike of a largemouth inhaling a popper can be contrasted with the subtle sip of a bluegill taking a rubber spider. Some surface patterns imitate frogs, injured baitfish, or insects, while others rely on noise and movement to entice strikes.

Foam surface patterns

Surface deer-hair patterns

Effective flies can be surprisingly simple to make, but can also be intricate and time consuming. We will look at both types.

There are many shapes and sizes of preformed foam bodies available for making surface patterns. They are durable, long lasting, and can be easily incorporated into surface design templates.

Both deer body and belly hair can be incorporated into many surface patterns. These materials are more time consuming (and messy) to work with, but allow for a wider range of creativity and color combining. Some anglers feel that hair bugs are more effective than foam because it has a more life-like feel to the fish when they grab it and they will hang on longer. Again, there are several basic design templates that are proven producers on the water.

Floating Spider/Ant

Hook: TMC 200R #10 for spider bodies; Daiichi 1310 #10 for ant bodies

Thread: UTC 70 Denier, color matched to body

Body: Preformed closed-cell foam, which can be found in various sizes and shapes in black, yellow, white, and chartreuse

Legs: White rubber hackle or legs

The completed Floating Spider and Floating Ant

1. Lay a base of thread over the hook shank, then move the thread to the halfway point on the hook.

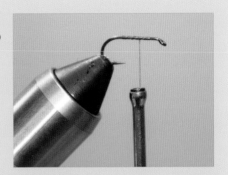

2. Put the foam body on top of the hook shank and tightly wrap thread over the body, holding it so that it will not spin off the top of the hook.

3. Tie down a rubber leg strand on each side of the body so that they form a V shape on each side when wrapped tightly.

4. Move the thread in front of the foam and tie off. Be sure to secure the thread wrapping the body and legs with superglue.

POPPERS

Simple Popper

Hook: Mustad Signature C52SBLN, sized to popper body
Thread: UTC 140 Denier
Tail: Gray squirrel tail
Flash: Pearl Cascade Crest Krinkle Mirror Flash
Body: Preformed closed-cell foam popper
Legs (optional): Round rubber

1. Put a base of thread on the hook shank and coat with superglue. Make sure the popper has a predrilled hole through the center of the body.

2. Slide the popper on the hook, flat side down, through the predrilled hole. Make sure there is an adequate gap between the point of the hook and the popper body for fish to be hooked.

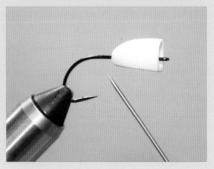

3. Tie in squirrel tail and flash.

4. Rubber legs can be added if desired. The thread needs to be tied off behind the popper, making the use of a whip finisher necessary.

Note: Preformed closed-cell foam popper bodies come in different sizes and assorted colors. They should be sized to the hook you are using. White bodies can be colored with a permanent marker.

Instant Popper

The Instant Popper

Hook: TMC 8089, #6 or #10
Thread: UTC 140 or 70 Denier, depending on hook size
Tail: Arctic fox with Holographic Flashabou
Body: Spirit River Instant Bass Bug, sized to hook

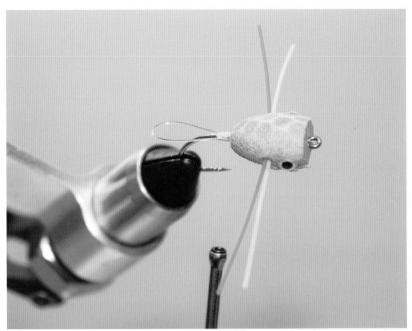

A mono loop can be added to prevent soft tailing materials from tangling in the hook when cast.

Note: Spirit River's Instant Bass Bug bodies are available in different colors and several sizes. They are glued onto the hook shank the same as other popper bodies. To keep softer tail materials from tangling in the hook when cast, a loop of 12- to 15-pound monofilament can be tied on the shank before the tail material is added.

Blockhead Popper

Blockhead poppers have a wider surface area in front and make considerably more noise than a round popper. They can draw fish from a farther distance.

Hook: Mustad 3366, #1
Thread: UTC 140 Denier
Tail: Spirit River Jailhouse Marabou with Holographic Flashabou
Body: Rainy's Blockhead Popper Head, large
Weed guard: 20-pound monofilament

1. In order to attach the blockhead body to the hook, a cut is made down the middle of the body from the flat side.

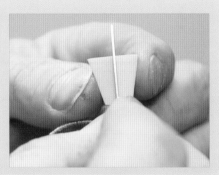

The cut needs to be nearly as deep as the back part of the body.

2. Attach the weed guard and cover the hook shank with the thread up close to the eye and back. The thread-covered hook shank is inserted into the cut.

3. Carefully brush or squeeze superglue into the cut and squeeze both sides together until set.

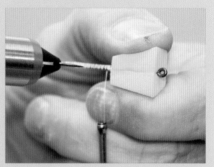

4. Add tail material and tie off weed guard as described in chapter 3.

Note: Blockhead Popper Heads are available in several sizes and colors. A variety of other materials such as arctic fox tail and Extra Select Craft Fur can be used for the tail, and rubber legs can be added if desired.

Simple Slider

By turning the popper body used in the previous pattern backward, we can make a slider-style head. We can also use bucktail for the tail on either the popper or slider. The slider head does not make noise but will dart side to side like an injured baitfish.

Hook: Mustad Signature C52SBLN, sized to popper body
Thread: UTC 140 Denier
Tail: Bucktail with Holographic Flashabou
Body: Preformed closed-cell foam popper, reversed

The Simple Slider

Divers

Rabbit Strip Diver

Divers are designed to pull a few inches under the water when retrieved. They also leave a bubble trail and make a bit of noise to attract fish. This is the simplest pattern to make that incorporates deer body hair. It needs to be a part of the arsenal of every serious bass angler. As they are usually fished near cover, a weed guard is necessary. Key colors are black, olive, chartreuse, and white.

Hook: Mustad 3366, #1 to #4
Thread: UTC 140 Denier
Tail: Rabbit Zonker Strip
Flash: Holographic Flashabou
Head: Deer body hair
Weed guard: 20-pound monofilament

1. Attach the weed guard and tie down a rabbit strip approximately 4 inches long plus flash in the middle of the hook shank.

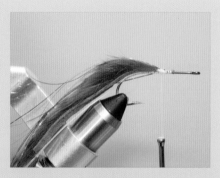

2. Cut a section of deer belly hair about the diameter of a pencil right at the hide. Pull out all the loose hair and fuzzy underfur and trim the butt ends even so that the length of the hair section is about 2 inches.

3. Hold the deer hair on top of the hook shank and make a loose wrap over top of it, then make another wrap and tighten down on the hair, letting it flair out in the back and front. Wrap the thread forward through the butt ends, then with the hair packer, push the hair tight to the back and make a few wraps of thread in front of the hair.

4. Repeat the process until you reach the hook eye (it will probably take 3 bunches of hair to fill the shank), then tie off and cut the thread.

5. Trim the hair flat on the bottom of the hook shank.

6. Trim the hair shorter and narrower at the hook eye, tapering wider to the rear. Be sure to leave a collar of longer hair. Restart the thread and tie off the weed guard.

Hairy Diver

A drawback of Rabbit Strip Divers is the water weight they pick up, making larger ones difficult to cast. Using Icelandic sheep hair for the tail helps solve this problem. This material has bulk and great movement in the water, but compresses to nothing out of the water, allowing larger patterns to be picked up off the water and cast easily. Icelandic sheep is available in a wide range of colors and can also be accented with permanent markers.

Hook: Gamakatsu B10S, #2/0 or #1/0
Thread: UTC 210 or 140 Denier, depending on hook size
Tail: Icelandic sheep hair, single color or layered colors
Flash: Holographic Flashabou
Head: Deer belly hair
Weed guard: 20-pound monofilament

The Hairy Diver

A Dynamic Duo

Froggy Diver

Few flies define fly fishing for largemouth bass like a frog-pattern, deer-hair diver. If I had to put one fly in my box to chase largemouth, this would be it.

Frog patterns can be quite intricate and time consuming to tie. Much of this is for the benefit of the angler and adds nothing to the fish-catching effectiveness of the fly. The simple, stripped-down version given here can be quickly mastered by a beginner and will catch fish.

Hook: Gamakatsu #65110 Wire Guard Worm Hook, #2/0 to #2 (Any of the wide-gap hooks listed are usable, but a weed guard will need to be tied in.)
Thread: UTC 210 or 140 Denier, depending on hook size, olive
Tail: White or tan arctic fox tail or marabou
Legs: White, chartreuse, then olive large neck hackles
Head: White, chartreuse, then olive deer belly hair

1. With the hook in the vise, open up the weed guard so that there is room to access the shank. Start the thread behind the wire holding the weed guard and wrap back to the bend.

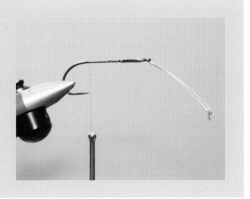

2. Add the arctic fox tail or marabou, then gauge the length of the first (white) neck hackle at about twice the length of the hook shank.

3. Cut the hackle and trim short several barbules on each side of the center shaft.

4. With the trimmed part of the hackle right where the tail was tied in, tie down on the side of the hook shank so that the hackle curves toward you.

5. Repeat the process with a chartreuse then olive neck hackle. Do the same on the opposite side of the hook. Coat the thread holding the hackles with superglue and let dry. The neck hackles represent the kicking legs of a swimming frog.

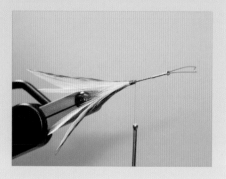

6. Prepare and tie in a section of white deer belly hair as was done for both the Hairy Diver and Rabbit Strip Diver. Tie the deer hair as we did in previous diver patterns—tips to the rear and made to flare in front.

7. Repeat with a section of chartreuse belly hair, then fill the rest of the shank with olive belly hair. It should take 3 or 4 total sections of belly hair to fill the shank.

8. Tie off and cut the thread, then trim the hair into a wide, tapered frog-shaped head. Pinch the weed guard back into position over the hook point.

Note: Various types of eyes can be added, but really do not enhance the fish-catching properties of this fly. They are more for decorative purposes, though 8mm plastic doll eyes may add some buoyancy and aid floatation slightly. The deer-hair head of the fly can be treated with a spray or paste floatant to help keep it on the surface. Flash can be added with the tail as desired.

Froggy Popper

When a bit more noise is needed to trigger strikes on the surface, a frog popper can fill the bill. As this is the last pattern to be presented, it is also the most intricate that we will tie. The same materials and tying sequence is used as in the diver, but the deer belly hair will be prepared and tied in differently. The trimming of the hair will also be different.

Hook: Gamakatsu B10S, #1/0 to #2
Thread: UTC 140 Denier, chartreuse
Tail: White or tan arctic fox or marabou, with white then olive large neck hackles on each side
Legs (optional): Cascade Crest Lizard Legs or other rubber hackle
Body: White, chartreuse, then olive deer belly hair
Weed guard: 20-pound monofilament

1. The weed guard is tied in and the tail and hackles attached as in the Froggy Diver. Two neck hackles are adequate in this application, as they are not as critical as in the diver version.

2. Cut a portion of white deer belly hair about the diameter of a pencil close to the hide of the piece of hair. Clean out all the underfur and shorter hairs, then drop the hair, tips first, into the hair evener.

3. Tap the hair evener several times on a hard surface to even the tips of the deer belly hair. Remove the insert tube from the hair evener and pull the hair out by the butt ends.

4. Leave the tips even and uncut, and trim the hair to about 1½ inches in length.

5. Hold the hair over the hook shank, tips to the rear, and tie down so that about 1 inch sticks back behind the thread. Make several additional wraps through the butt ends, then push the butt ends back with the hair packing tool.

6. Cut and clean a section of chartreuse deer belly hair. This time cut off both the tips and the butt ends straight across so that the length of the hair is about 1½ inches. Lay the hair on top of the hook and make a loose wrap of thread over the hair.

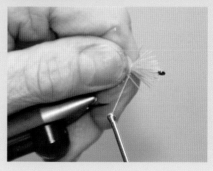

7. Continue to wrap the thread and while increasing pressure, let the hair slip out of your fingers and spin around the hook shank.

8. Wrap the thread until the hair stops spinning, then take the thread in front of the hair and pack it back as tight as you can.

9. This process is repeated down the hook shank with additional chartreuse then olive belly hair to fill the shank of the hook, making sure that each section of hair is tightly packed before the next one is added. Optional legs can be added by tying 3 rubber legs in between hair sections with a crisscross wrap.

10. Same as step 9. Rubber legs, if added, are tied in on the forward part of the hook shank.

11. When the eye of the hook is reached, tie off and cut the thread.

12. Remove the fly from the vise and trim the hair on the bottom as close to the shank as possible to open up the gap of the hook.

13. Trim the hair so that it tapers from wide and high at the front to smaller toward the back of the fly. Take care not to cut the rubber legs if they were tied in. Then trim the rubber legs shorter and evenly on both sides.

14. Put the fly back in the vise and tie off the weed guard.

INDEX

Ambloplites rupestris, 4, 6

Baitfish Bugger Variation, The, 67
barbell eyes, tying, 48–49
Basic Deep Minnow, The, 74–77
Basic Woolly Bugger, The, 59–62
Bead-Head or Cone-Head Variation,
    68–69
beads, 37
Better Bugger Variation, The,
    62–64
black crappie, 7
Blockhead Popper, 89–90
bluegill, 1, 4–6
bobbins, 19–20
bobbin threaders, 22
bodies, 28–29, 38–39, 46–47, 82
bodkins, 21
bream/brim (bluegill), 1, 4–6

Clouser, Bob, 74
cones, 37
Coosa bass, 4
Crafty Minnow, 79
crappie, 1, 6–7

Damsel/Dragon Variation, The,
    65–66
Deep Minnow Family, The
    Basic Deep Minnow, The,
        74–77
    Crafty Minnow, 79
    Fish Head Minnow, 80
    Jig Deep Minnow, 78
    overview, 74
    Perch Minnow Variation, 78
    Simple Minnow, 79
    Spottail Shiner Variation, 77

divers
    Froggy Diver, 95–97
    Hairy Diver, 94
    Rabbit Strip Diver, 92–93
Dobsonfly larvae, 70

equipment, fly-fishing, 9–13
eyes, 35–37, 48–49

feathers, 30–31
Feenstra, Kevin, 12
fish, warm-water, 1–8
Fish Head Minnow, 80
flash, 35, 37
flies. *See also* fly tying, overview;
    specific names of flies
    casting effectiveness and size
        of, 10
    definition and overview, 12–13
floaters, weight-forward, 9
Floating Spider/Ant, 83–84
fly tying, overview
    basic techniques, 41–53
    materials for, 25–39
    subsurface patterns, 55
    surface patterns, 81–82
    tools for, 15–23
foam, as preformed bodies, 38–39,
    82
Froggy Diver, 95–97
Froggy Popper, 98–101
fur, animal, 34

green sunfish, 4
Guadalupe bass, 4

hackle pliers, 20–21
hackles, 30–31

hair
    animal, 32–33, 82
    synthetic, 34–35
hair packers, 23
hair stackers, 23
Hairy Diver, 94
half-hitch tools, 21
Hellgrammite Variation, The, 70
herl, 29
hooks, 26–27, 50–51

Instant Poppers, 87–88

Jig Deep Minnow, 78

Kentucky bass, 4

largemouth bass, 1–3, 9,
    11, 12
leaders, 9, 11, 12
legs, 38, 39
Lepomis cyanellus, 4
Lepomis gulosus, 4
Lepomis macrochirus, 1, 4–6
Lepomis megolotis, 4
Lepomis microlophus, 4
lighting, 24
lines, 9, 10–11
longear sunfish, 4

marabou feathers, 21
medallions, 63
Micropterus dolomieu, 3–4, 10,
    11, 12
Micropterus punctulatus, 4
Micropterus salmoides, 1–3, 9,
    11, 12
Morone americana, 8
Morone chrysops, 1, 7–8

Perch Minnow Variation, 78
Pomoxis anularis, 7
Pomoxis nigromaculatus, 7

poppers
    Blockhead Popper, 89–90
    Froggy Popper, 98–101
    Instant Poppers, 87–88
    Simple Popper, 85–86
    Simple Slider, 91

Rabbit Strip Diver, 92–93
redear sunfish, 4
reels, 9–10, 12
rock bass, 4, 6
rods, 9, 11, 12

sand bass, 1, 7–8
scissors, 18–19
Sculpin Bugger, 72–73
shellcracker, 4
shoal bass, 4
silver bass, 1, 7–8
Simple Crayfish, 70–71
Simple Minnow, 79
Simple Popper, 85–86
Simple Slider, 91
Sinking Spider, The, 56–58
Sinking Spider variation, 59
sinking tips, 10, 11
smallmouth bass, 3–4, 10, 11, 12
speckled perch (specks, speckles), 7
spot, 4
Spottail Shiner Variation, 77
spotted bass, 4
sunfish, 1, 4

tackle, 9–13
tails, animal, 31–32
thread
    finishing off the, 44–45
    overview of material, 27–28
    starting the, 41–42
    wrapping the, 43
tippets, 9, 11
tweezers, 23

ultraviolet (UV) materials, 25

vises, 15–18

warmouth, 4
weedless hooks, 27, 50–51
weights, 10, 12, 38, 46–47
whip finishers, 22–23
whip finishes, 52–53
white bass, 1, 7–8
white crappie, 7
white perch, 8
Woolly Bugger Family, The
  Baitfish Bugger Variation, The, 67
  Basic Woolly Bugger, The, 59–62

Bead-Head or Cone-Head
  Variation, 68–69
Better Bugger Variation, The,
  62–64
Damsel/Dragon Variation, The,
  65–66
Hellgrammite Variation, The, 70
Sculpin Bugger, 72–73
Simple Crayfish, 70–71
Sinking Spider variation, 59
work areas, 24–25

yellow perch, 1, 7

ABOUT THE AUTHOR

Jerry Darkes is a well-known Great Lakes area fly fisherman and guide. He has over 40 years of experience in fresh and salt water, has been featured in several books and films about Great Lakes area fly fishing, and has authored numerous articles on a variety of fly fishing subjects. He is also a fly tier with numerous patterns to his credit and is recognized as a speaker and instructor throughout the area.